AF599114

COOL CARS
CHEVROLET
CORVETTE
Z06
EPIC
BY KAITLYN DULING
BELLWETHER MEDIA ››› MINNEAPOLIS, MN

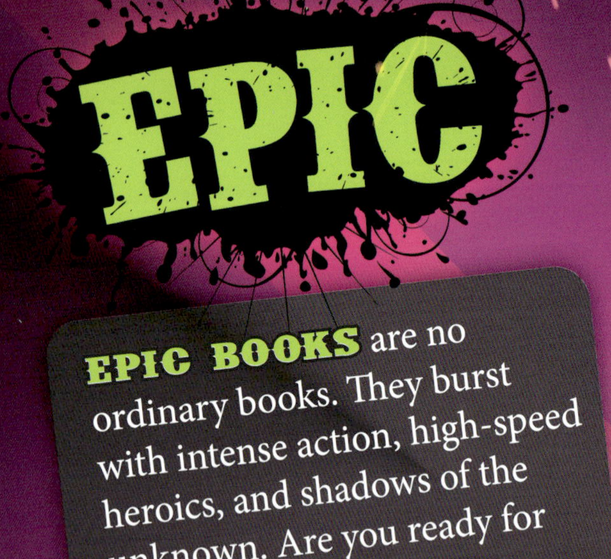

EPIC BOOKS are no ordinary books. They burst with intense action, high-speed heroics, and shadows of the unknown. Are you ready for an Epic adventure?

This edition first published in 2025 by Bellwether Media, Inc.

Library of Congress Cataloging-in-Publication Data

Names: Duling, Kaitlyn, author.
Title: Chevrolet Corvette Z06 / by Kaitlyn Duling.
Description: Minneapolis, MN : Bellwether Media, Inc., [2025] | Series: Epic. Cool cars | Includes bibliographical references and index. | Audience: Ages 7-12 | Audience: Grades 2-3 |
Summary: "Engaging images accompany information about the Chevrolet Corvette Z06. The combination of high-interest subject matter and light text is intended for students in grades 2 through 7" -- Provided by publisher.
Identifiers: LCCN 2024002266 (print) | LCCN 2024002267 (ebook) | ISBN 9798893040524 (library binding) | ISBN 9781644879924 (ebook) Subjects: LCSH: Corvette automobile--Juvenile literature
Classification: LCC TL215.C6 D85 2025 (print) | LCC TL215.C6 (ebook) | DDC 629.222/2--dc23/eng/20240205
LC record available at https://lccn.loc.gov/2024002266
LC ebook record available at https://lccn.loc.gov/2024002267

Editor: Rachael Barnes Designer: Jeffrey Kollock

Printed in the United States of America, North Mankato, MN.

TABLE OF CONTENTS

ROAD RACER

The driver presses the gas pedal. The car screams! It gets louder as it speeds up.

People hear the Chevrolet Corvette Z06 coming. It races by with style!

ALL ABOUT THE CORVETTE Z06

Chevrolet began in Detroit, Michigan, in 1911. It is often called Chevy.

Chevy sells cars around the world. The Camaro and the Bel Air are famous **models**.

CAMARO ZL1s

People could buy a Z06 **options package**. The package made cars race-ready!

The Corvette Z06 returned as its own model in 2001.

LIMITED RUN

Only 199 Corvette Z06s were built in 1963. Today, they are hard to find!

1963 CORVETTES

CORVETTE Z06 BASICS

YEAR FIRST MADE	2001
COST	starts around $112,700
HOW MANY MADE	over 5,000 in 2023

FEATURES

V8 engine

side inlets

rear spoiler

The 2023 is the fifth Z06 model. It was built in Kentucky.

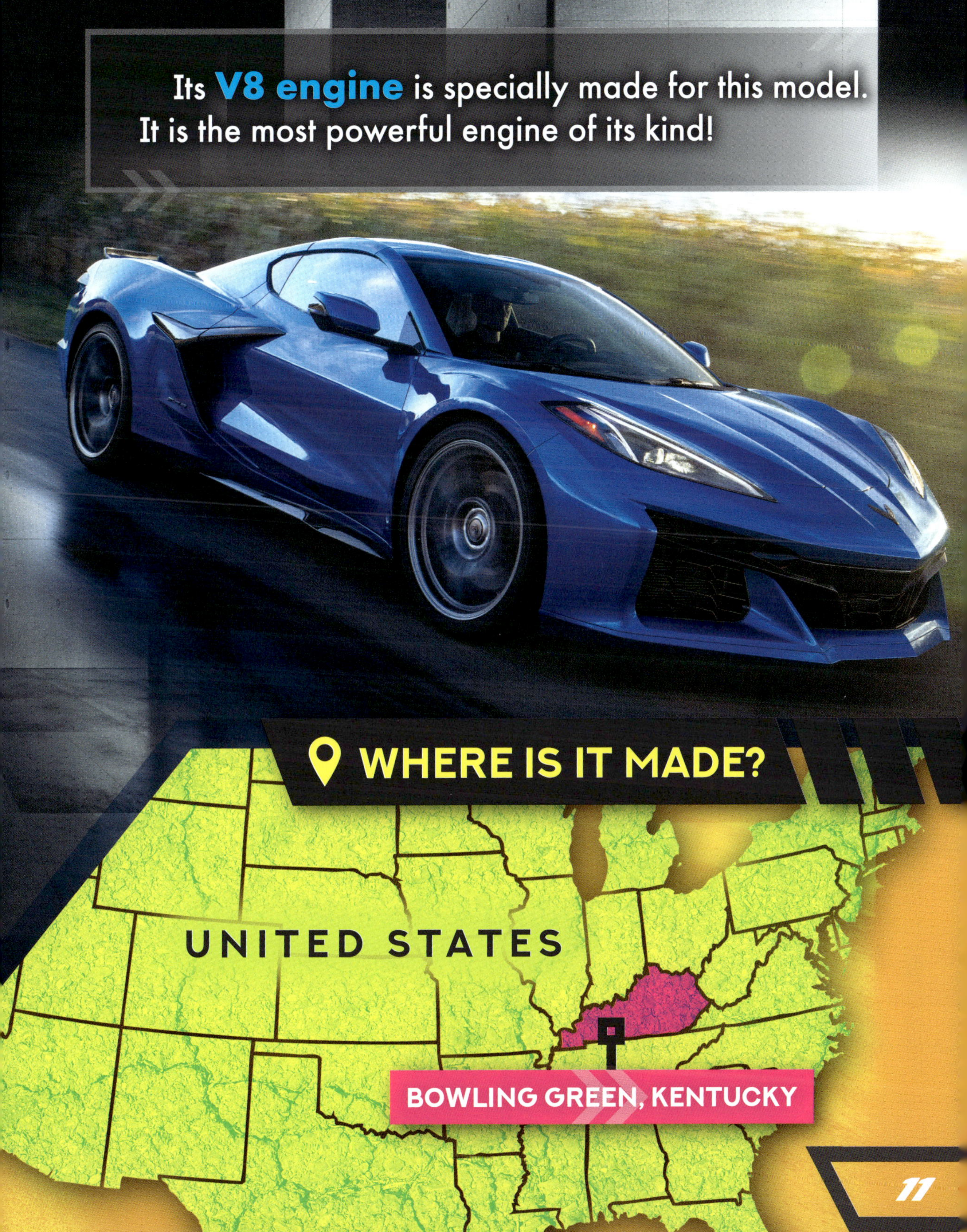
Its **V8 engine** is specially made for this model. It is the most powerful engine of its kind!
WHERE IS IT MADE?
UNITED STATES
BOWLING GREEN, KENTUCKY

PARTS OF THE CORVETTE Z06

The Corvette Z06's engine is in the middle of the car. Engine noises roar out of the **exhaust barrels**.

The car has a trunk in the front. It is known as a frunk!

ENGINE SPECS

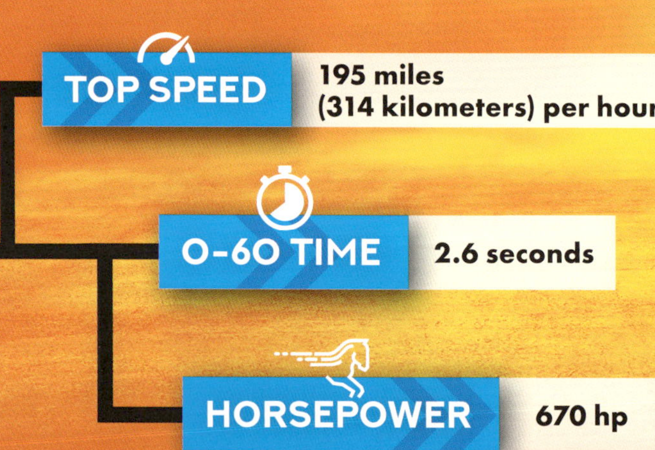

FRUNK
CORVETTE
EXHAUST BARRELS

The car is **aerodynamic**. It is lower and wider than past models. **Side inlets** help air move through the car.

SIDE INLET

SIZE CHART

WIDTH 79.7 inches (202.4 centimeters)

Its rear **spoiler** helps the car grip the road.

A special Z06 was released in 2023. It honors the Corvette's 70th birthday!

CONVERTIBLE

70TH BIRTHDAY MODEL

The Corvette Z06 can be built as a **coupe** or a **convertible**. The convertible's roof can fold down. A button on the **key fob** controls it.

Buyers can pick different roof styles. One is see-through!

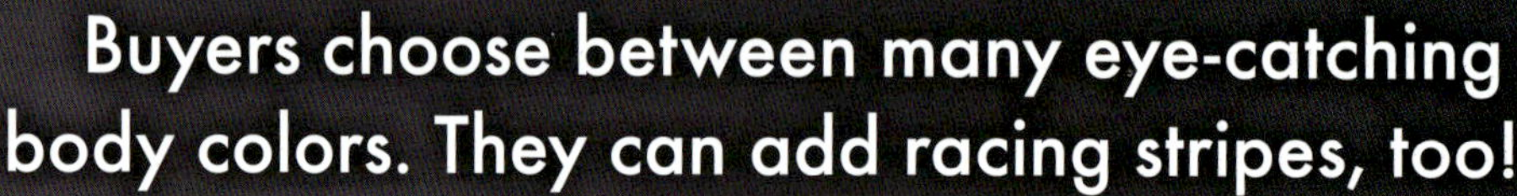

Buyers choose between many eye-catching body colors. They can add racing stripes, too!

WATCH WHERE YOU'RE GOING

Buyers can add a data recorder to their car. It saves videos. It records braking and lap times.

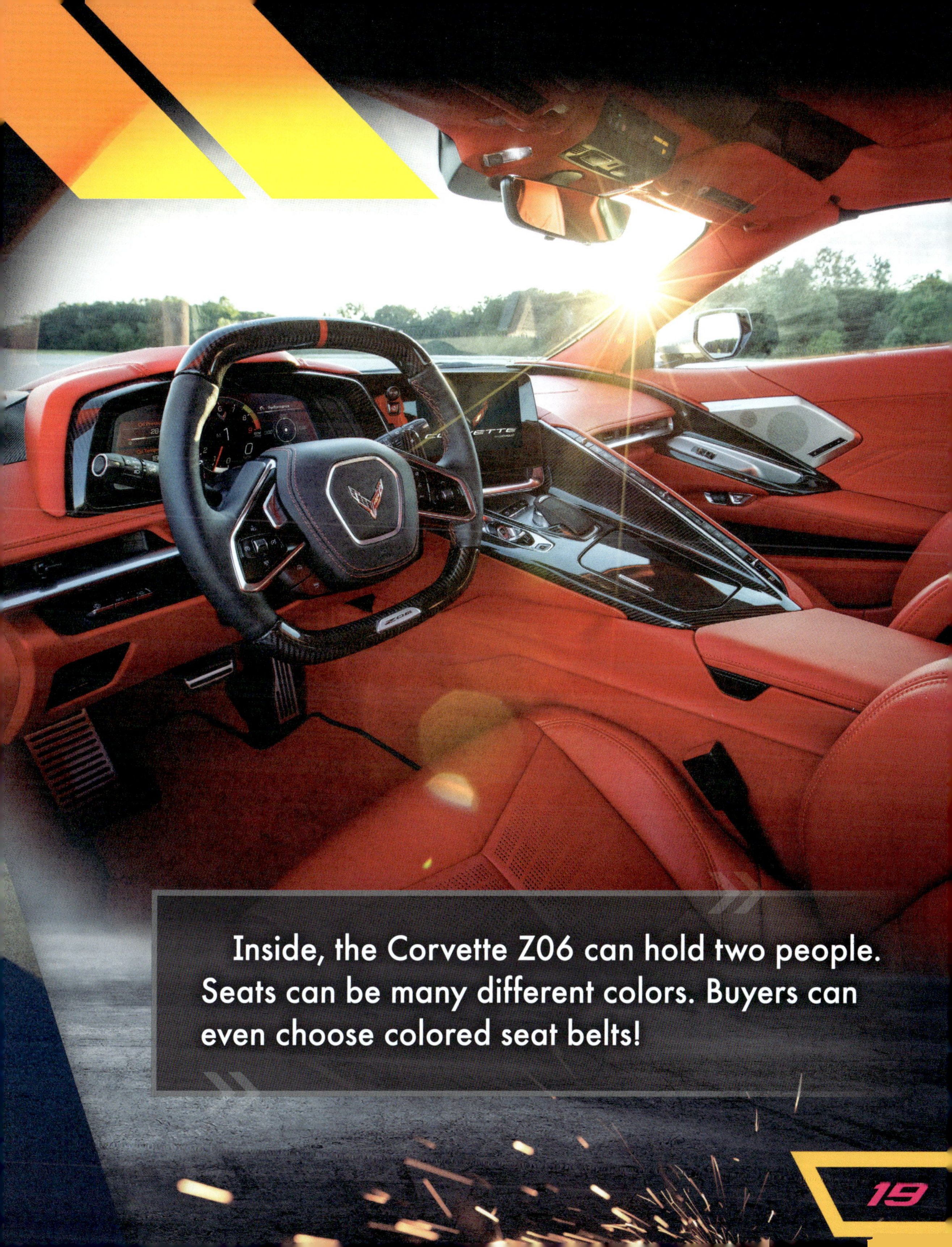

Inside, the Corvette Z06 can hold two people. Seats can be many different colors. Buyers can even choose colored seat belts!

THE CORVETTE Z06'S FUTURE

The next Z06 is a track-only model. The Corvette Z06 GT3.R hit the racetrack in 2024. This car may be the last gas-powered V8 Corvette. Many future Chevy cars will be **electric**!

CORVETTE Z06 GT3.R

GLOSSARY

aerodynamic—able to move through air easily

convertible—a car with a folding or soft roof

coupe—a car with a hard roof that often has two doors

electric—able to run without gasoline

exhaust barrels—pipes used to direct gases and sounds from a car's engine out and away from the car

key fob—a small remote used to control some functions of a car

models—specific kinds of cars

options package—a group of features that can be added to a car for an extra cost

side inlets—openings on the sides of a car's body that allow air to enter and exit

spoiler—a part on the back of a car that helps a car grip the road

V8 engine—an engine with 8 cylinders arranged in the shape of a "V"

TO LEARN MORE

AT THE LIBRARY

Emminizer, Theresa. *Corvettes.* Buffalo, N.Y.: Enslow Publishing, 2023.

Garstecki, Julia. *Corvette Z06.* Mankato, Minn.: Black Rabbit Books, 2020.

Sommer, Nathan. *Chevrolet Corvette Stingray.* Minneapolis, Minn.: Bellwether Media, 2023.

ON THE WEB

FACTSURFER

Factsurfer.com gives you a safe, fun way to find more information.

1. Go to www.factsurfer.com.
2. Enter "Chevrolet Corvette Z06" into the search box and click 🔍.
3. Select your book cover to see a list of related content.

INDEX

The images in this book are reproduced through the courtesy of: Chevrolet, front cover, pp. 3, 4, 5, 7, 8, 9 (isolated, engine, inlet, and spoiler), 10, 11, 12, 13 (main), 14 (main), 15 (main and length), 16, 17, 18, 19, 20, 21; J.A. Dunbar, p. 6; Sarah Stierch, p. 13 (frunk); Erik Drost/ Wikipedia, p. 14 (width).